#1

"I trust you're better at this than I would be."

#2

"You seem like the expert here—take the lead!"

#3

"I'd handle this, but you're closer to it."

#4

"This is a great growth opportunity for you."

#5

"You have the context, so I'll let you run with it."

#6

"Let me empower you to take this on."

#7

"I'd do it, but I don't want to steal your thunder."

#8

"I know how much you love challenges—this one's all yours!"

#9

"You've got this. I believe in you."

#10

"Why don't you handle this, and I'll review it later?"

#11

"Let's divide and conquer. You do the hard part."

#12

"You're the only one who can truly pull this off."

#13

"I'd do it myself, but I think you'll do it faster."

#14

"I'm delegating this because I know you'll crush it."

#15

"This task has your name written all over it."

#16

"You've got the vision for this. Go make it happen."

#17

"Let me know when it's done, and I'll approve it."

#18

"You're great at figuring these things out."

#19

"I'd explain, but you'll figure it out better than I could."

#20

"I trust your instincts on this one."

#21

"Can you take the first pass? I'll finesse it later."

#22

"I'd love your creative input on this."

#23

"Why don't you lead this, and I'll stay in the loop?"

#24

"This feels like a project you'd shine in."

#25

"You're the subject matter expert here."

#26

"This aligns perfectly with your skill set."

#27

"I'm delegating because you're better at the details."

#28

"I know how much you love taking initiative."

#29

"I think this task needs your magic touch."

#30

"You're better at handling ambiguity than I am."

#31

"This is right up your alley!"

#32

"You'd do a better job than I ever could."

#33

"Take a crack at this, and I'll weigh in later."

34

"You've got the bandwidth for this, right?"

#35

"This feels like a perfect fit for your talents."

#36

"You're the most qualified person for this."

#37

"I'd help, but I don't want to step on your toes."

#38

"You'll nail this one for sure."

#39

"This is your chance to show everyone your expertise."

#40

"You're the go-to person for things like this."

#41

"I'm passing this to you because I'm stretched too thin."

#42

"I'm counting on you to make sense of this."

#43

"You're always great at these sorts of tasks."

#44

"I have a feeling you'll knock this out of the park."

#45

"You're better at managing these complexities."

#46

"Let me delegate this to the best person for the job—you."

#47

"This aligns with your goals, doesn't it?"

#48

"I'm assigning this to you because you're a quick learner."

#49

"You'll probably have this done before I even figure it out."

#50

"I'm confident this task is in good hands with you."

www.ingramcontent.com/pod-product-compliance
Lightning Source LLC
Chambersburg PA
CBHW070946220526
45471CB00007B/2917